What People Are Saying about
The Daily Edge

"David's book is a quick read that could change the efficiency in your entire life! This transformation will leave you with more time!"

—Steven Schussler, founder of Rain Forest Café,
author of *It's a Jungle out There*

"*The Daily Edge* is the proverbial 'spoon full of sugar' for productivity ailments! David's tips are easy to digest and offer a variety of sound tactics to affect positive change in all aspects of one's life."

—Karen Skirten, former Corporate President, Executive Women International

"If you're going to be successful in the C-Suite, you can't afford to waste one day, one minute, or one encounter. David Horsager gives you the edge you need to be at the top of the business food chain."

—Jeffrey Hayzlett, primetime television and radio show host and
bestselling author of *The Mirror Test* and *Running the Gauntlet*

"David is simply the best at explaining useful tips and methods in understandable and engaging ways. Get *The Daily Edge*!"

—Marcy T. Rogers, M.Ed., President and CEO, SpineMark

"David takes the skills of the successful and reveals in easy-to-follow strategies how to take control of your daily routine. Jump start your career by devouring this book now. I highly recommend it!"

—"Famous Dave" Anderson, founder of Famous Dave's of America, Inc.

"Powerful and actionable, this guide gives you practical tips you can use right away! Leap to the next level with these strategies."

—Rory Vaden, *New York Times* bestselling author of *Take the Stairs*

"David is right on. His tips are simple, applicable and powerful. His technique to dive deeper until you have a clear action plan is brilliant!"

—Jill Blashack Strahan, CEO, Tastefully Simple

"As a professor looking for that competitive advantage for my students, David brings common sense into common practice. As a leading expert in trust, David now expands into the area of productivity. My students will have the 'edge' when it comes to their professional development."

—Dr. Karel Sovak, Associate Professor, Gary Tharaldson School of Business

"These strategies are as clear and usable as they are wise."

—Willis Turner, President and CEO,
Sales & Marketing Executives International, Inc.

"*The Daily Edge* challenges personal growth and provides a blueprint for organizational trust and productivity. We use David's strategies in our football program to build strong habits essential to leadership both on and off the field."

—Peter Haugen, Head Football Coach, Gustavus Adolphus College

"Skyline Technology Solutions uses David's national bestseller *The Trust Edge* and we can testify to the difference it makes. We're eager to get *The Daily Edge* into everyone's hands and see its impact in our organization."

—Anthony F. Diekemper, CEO, Skyline Technology Solutions

"*The Daily Edge* is a sure-fire hit to keep your team positive and working on trust-building actions. His quick tips and strategies plant the seed for you to cultivate and harvest for years to come!"

—Kent M. Senf, COO, C&B Operations

"Horsager balances two seemingly opposing objectives—maximizing productivity and maintaining healthy relationships. Any leader who wants to experience this balance must get this book!"

—Dr. Alan Zimmerman, author of *The Payoff Principle: Discover the 3 Secrets for Getting What You Want Out of Life and Work*

"David Horsager's common sense approach to managing time has inspired me to be more efficient in my work and everyday tasks."

—Mike Hajek, Director of Contracts and Marketing,
National Joint Powers Alliance

THE
DAILY
EDGE

THE
DAILY
EDGE

*Simple Strategies
to Increase Efficiency
and Make an Impact
Every Day*

DAVID HORSAGER

Author of the National Bestseller
THE TRUST EDGE

BK

Berrett–Koehler Publishers, Inc.
a BK Business book

Berrett-Koehler Publishers, Inc.
1333 Broadway, Suite 1000
Oakland, CA 94612-1921
Tel: (510) 817-2277 Fax: (510) 817-2278 www.bkconnection.com

Printed by Network TwentyOne International, Inc. 2015. Rights assigned by Berrett-Koehler Publishers, Inc., 1333 Broadway, Suite 1000, Oakland, CA 94612.

Berrett-Koehler and the BK logo are registered trademarks of Berrett-Koehler Publishers, Inc.

Printed in the United States of America

Library of Congress Cataloging-in-Publication Data
Horsager, David.
The daily edge : simple strategies to increase efficiency and make an impact every day / by David Horsager.—First edition.
    pages cm
ISBN 978-1-62656-595-1 (hardcover)
1. Time management. 2. Industrial efficiency. I. Title.
HD69.T54H6633 2015
650.1'1—dc23
                    2015021642

FIRST EDITION

20 19 18 17 16 15   10 9 8 7 6 5 4 3 2 1

Project manager and copyeditor: Heidi Sheard
Cover designer, text designer, and compositor: Heidi Koopman/Purpose Design

Dedication

To Nate, who has the Daily Edge,
but not at the expense of relationships.

To Lisa, who manages
our home and four children
with diligence and grace.

Simple Strategies

Acknowledgments

Audience members and clients have inspired the writing of this book, and many others have helped bring it to completion. I thank my close friends and advisors Loren Horsager, Joe Kimbell, Scott Lundeen, and Jason Sheard. A big thank you to the two Heidi's on my team. Heidi Sheard is a dear friend and my wonderful editor. Heidi Koopman is my fantastic designer who captured my vision on this project and took it to yet another level. Thanks to Jeevan Sivasubramaniam and the incredible team at Berrett-Koehler Publishers. Heartfelt gratitude to my core team, Ryan Naylor, Reid Velo, and Anne Engstrom—they are trusted colleagues and fulfill our mission at Horsager Leadership, Inc. with passion, integrity, and humility. I am grateful to God for my amazing wife Lisa and my four children who support and inspire me every day.

Thank you to the organizations and audiences who have invited me to speak and consult—many of you inspired, tested, and ultimately revealed the level of productivity that comes when one has *The Daily Edge*.

The Daily Edge *(n)*: The advantage or edge gained when priorities are clear and there is a daily effort to act on those priorities.

The inspiration for this book came from learning and implementing several techniques that radically changed the way I do work and live life. It all started when I took some time off. I began reading several books on productivity and time management, which made me become more aware of how people use their time. I watched a great leader use time so effectively, yet, not at the expense of relationships. Those experiences inspired me to develop and implement the techniques featured in this book.

While I never intended to be a productivity expert, people who attend my presentations and seminars have asked me to expand on this topic of productivity. Perhaps one of the reasons why my message is appealing is the simplicity of my approach. This book is unique in that it isn't long on theories or philosophical ideas. Instead, it is packed with tips that I've gathered and used in my own life. They have made a huge difference for me, and they can do the same for you.

The Daily Edge will provide you with practical ways to be more efficient and effective while honoring relationships. Each of the tips has been passed on from a friend or learned from reflection after a busy day. Enjoy!

Tip 1

90-Day Quick Plan

Eighteen years ago a man challenged me to not complain for 90 days straight. I couldn't complain about anything, not food, not the weather, nothing. That changed my life. Some people say you can change a habit in 21 days. I question whether that is long enough. While 21 days may be too short, an entire year is too long. Think about it, most people can't keep their New Year's resolutions for even two weeks. People often think, "I have all year to get going on that." 90 days is a sweet spot. It is a short enough time frame to stay absolutely focused, and yet it is long enough to get more done than most people get done in a whole year. When I lost my weight, the first 90 days were the most important. In those three months, I lost thirty-three pounds, but more importantly, my thinking about food, exercise, and how I spent my time was transformed. Everything changed in 90 days.

Most strategic planning is done at an off-site retreat, yet provides little momentum toward action. Instead of an annual planning session, try making a 90-Day Quick Plan. Every 90 days we encourage everyone on our team to create a 90-Day Quick Plan. It gives leaders and teams an actionable framework that provides clarity and leads to tangible results both personally and professionally.

Here's how to make it work. Pick an area of your business or life that you'd like to address, and then ask six questions. *The plan should take less than 30 minutes to create.*

Question 1: *Where am I?* If you do not know where you are today, you cannot know where you would like to be in the future. (If you are doing a 90-Day Quick Plan as a team, ask, "Where are we?" and use "we" in the following questions as well.) Ask this question and you will be able to quickly identify strengths, weaknesses, opportunities, and threats. For example, where am I in my relationship with my kids? Where am I in my health? Where am I in comparison to expected sales? Where are we as far as the number of people we are reaching with our message or product?

Question 2: *Where am I going in 90 days?* Remember, it is not one year or five years like many strategic plans. Thinking about your answer in question 1, where would you like to be in 90 days? Write a clear, quantifiable (numerical if possible) goal. You will likely accomplish more than you thought in just 90 days!

Question 3: *Why am I going?* If the "why" is strong enough, the plan does not need to be perfect. If a building is burning and my kids are in it, I don't need to know every detail—I'm going in because my "why" is so strong. When your team is motivated and unified, they'll do the little things differently. They'll stay passionate and focused, and they'll finish.

Question 4: *How are we going to get there?* How? Keep asking how? until your team commits to taking specific actions.

Question 5: *How are we going to get there?* I press people to ask how? until they have come up with a specific action they will take starting today or tomorrow at the latest.

Question 6: *How are we going to get there?* I have found people must ask how? at least three times before they are clear enough. It may take asking how? seven times in order to get enough clarity. The point is don't stop asking how until you or your team has decided on a specific action that will be taken starting today or tomorrow.

Making It Happen

I remember when I really got this idea of asking "how?" three times. I was training and consulting with one of the biggest heath care organizations in North America. They needed change! They were losing funding and patients. We were toward the end of our Trust Edge Experience. One hundred fifty top people including the CEO and senior leadership team were all seated at round tables. Each table had defined a specific challenge they were going to tackle. I remember asking one table full of top leaders about what they needed to take action on in order to grow and be more trusted. The table leader said, "We need to be clearer."

I said, "How will you be clearer?"

After brainstorming with his group, the table leader said, "We are going to communicate more."

I said, "How?"

After more brainstorming, he said, "We are going to hold each other accountable."

I said, "How?"

The table, seated with bright minds and fine leaders, had to be pushed three times in order to realize they needed a more specific action plan. They worked together to create a plan for communicating more often and more clearly. An important piece of their plan was how they were going to hold each other accountable to this effort. They were able to start following their plan the very next day.

On a personal level, when I decided to lose weight, I kept asking "how?" until I went from "eat less and exercise more" to defining fifteen specific actionable ideas I could implement on a daily basis.

With greater clarity around your 90-day plan, you will gain the trust of your team and bottom-line results will follow.

"The most pathetic person
in the world is someone who has sight
but no vision." —Helen Keller

 To watch David teach the 90-Day Quick Plan, go to www.youtube. com/watch?v=YQsZRU8TW-4

However beautiful
the **strategy**,
you should
occasionally look
at the **results**.

—Winston Churchill

Tip 2

DMA's:
Difference-Making
Actions

Have you ever had a day in which you worked really hard but felt like you didn't get anything done? Many people look at their to-do list and get so overwhelmed that they end up doing nothing! The DMA strategy gives powerful clarity. It works beautifully especially once you have your 90-Day Quick Plan. It was inspired by a strategy successfully used by Charles Schwab of Bethlehem Steel Company, the first American to earn a million-dollar annual salary.

DMA stands for Difference-Making Actions. DMA's simply give focus and intentionality to do the most important things every day. This simple strategy will increase results like nothing else. Make a habit of doing DMA's on a daily basis and your impact will multiply.

Here's how it works:

The DMA Strategy:

1. First thing every morning, take a sticky note.

2. At the top, write your most important current goal.

3. Then write the numbers 1-5 down the page.

4. Next to the 1, write the most important thing you could do today to accomplish that goal. Then write the next most important thing under 2, and so on.

5. You now have a list of the 5 most important things you could to today that would make the biggest difference in accomplishing your goal and ultimately fulfilling your organization's mission.

When you write your DMA's, make sure they are FUN:

F = First priority first. List your tasks in order of priority and then do them in order. Don't start working on the second task until you have finished the first one or you have come to a roadblock that requires someone else's help. Your DMA's are the most important actions for the day! Don't attempt more than five, or you might get overwhelmed and do nothing. If you can't boil them down to a few simply stated tasks, then you probably need to restate your goal.

U = Under the main vision and current major objective. DMA's are the five most important actions you can specifically take today to move your organization forward. They must come under your main vision and help accomplish your most important and current priorities!

N=Number attached. It is not a DMA unless there is a specific number attached. In other words "Calling more prospects" is not a DMA, but "Making 10 sales calls" is. "Organizing your office" is not a DMA, but "Organizing for 20 minutes" or "Cleaning out 2 drawers" are DMA's. Difference Making Actions must be quantifiable.

It is important to note that *DMA's are based solely on what you can do,* not what others need to do. In other words, "Calling three people" is a DMA as that does not rely on whether anyone answers or not. However, "Selling 5 gadgets" is not a DMA as it relies on what others must do. If you consistently do your DMA's, great outcomes will follow.

Each time you complete a Difference-Making Action, put a line through it. Believe it or not there is great satisfaction in seeing that sticky note at the end of the day with five lines crossed through your most important tasks. I once had an intern fresh out of college who was invaluable to our organization. Every day he accomplished his DMA's and then left that sticky note on his cubicle wall. Each day he added his next sticky note with lines through his accomplishments. Do you think he needed to be micromanaged? No way! There was proof on the wall he was doing Difference-Making Actions that moved our mission forward every single day.

Helpful DMA Hints

Be focused. When you write your DMA's, make sure that they are focused. Your DMA's are the most important actions for the day—you shouldn't have any more than three. If you can't boil them down to a few simply-stated tasks, then you probably need to restate your goal.

Be clear. Your DMA's should be clear and quantifiable. The focus here is on activities, not outcomes, so be sure you know exactly what you are going to do. "Make ten sales calls," or "spend one hour on the website" is much better than "sell more," or "work on the proposal."

Be realistic. Your DMA's will not be effective if you can't actually do them. Don't write down that you would like to write five proposals every day, if you know realistically you can't finish more than two.

Be committed. Lastly, build your day around them. Now that you have them, make sure you prioritize them over all other things, meetings, e-mails, and less important tasks. I often have my DMA's done by 11 a.m. because I do them first. The rest of my day can be structured as needed, but I first did something important that will make a significant impact on my organization and the lives of those we serve.

Example: A salesperson who wants to make $10,000 in commission every month might know from experience that he will need to find four new clients. And to find those four new clients, he needs to set one appointment each day, which he should be able to do by making 20 sales calls. He now has a strong DMA: Make 20 sales calls each morning. By making this the most important part of his day, he can learn to focus on that goal without being distracted by incoming phone calls, meetings, and other items that are urgent, but less important.

Never mistake motion for action.

—Ernest Hemingway

 To watch David teach the DMA strategy, go to www.youtube.com/watch?v=YCuxFKaTmIs

Simplicity

boils down to *two steps*:
Identify the
essential.
Eliminate the rest.

—Leo Babauta

Tip 3

Power Hour

1111

Writing down your DMA's is one thing, but getting them done is another. Despite our best intentions, we all know how quickly those priorities can be set aside in order to deal with the most urgent tasks.

In my office and many others, having a "power hour" has been a great way to keep at what is most important. It's so simple, you might be surprised at how well it works. So what is our secret? One quiet hour every day.

For 60 minutes each morning, we don't do meetings, phone calls, or e-mails. We don't take any interruptions. Messages go to voice mail and the inbox fills. Some would say, "You mean you won't take a call from a client to serve them?" No, we won't take a call during that hour so we can serve them even better. Unlike many offices, we can really focus, concentrate, and serve others best by actually getting something done for them. We focus on the activities we identified as most important to our long-term success.

Here's how to make it work for you:

- **Go public.** Let everyone you work with know you are setting aside an hour a day. Informing assistants, customers, and colleagues of your plans will leave them less likely to disturb you.

- **Share the idea.** In my office, everyone gets a quiet hour. That way, we don't interrupt each other, and we all get more done.

- **Be consistent.** Use the same time every day for your quiet hour if you can. It will allow people who work with you to get used to your routine and help reinforce the habit in your mind.

Try this method for a while, and I guarantee you will be surprised at how much you can accomplish in just 60 minutes. Not only will you make headway on your biggest projects, but you will find that by getting the day off to a strong start, you might feel energized to accomplish more in your remaining time.

Constantly distracted workers in busy offices
are able to focus on a task for an average of 11 minutes
before they're interrupted. —a University of California study

---

All things
are ready,
if our minds
be so.

—William Shakespeare

Tip 4

Focus

As a term, *multitasking* is a bit like *downsizing*—a nice word for something that is not really good for most people. Modern culture, with all of our technology and time-saving gadgets, has left us with a distorted view of productivity. Our image of productivity is the power executive handling two calls and a text message while wowing the big client at the same time. While that executive seems like a hero to most, the reality is that those sorts of habits are unproductive. Humans are simply more efficient and effective when they concentrate. That is, you can do five things better and faster by doing them one at a time, with your mind focused on each single task.

Learning to concentrate isn't complicated, but that doesn't mean it is easy. Most of us have years, and possibly decades, of bad habits to break.

Here's a start:

- **Focus.** It doesn't matter if you're working on the most important proposal of your life or an e-mail to your manager. You will do a better job if you're focused on what is right in front of you. Decide which task gets your attention and then focus on only that one until it is finished.

- **Eliminate distractions.** Cell phones, e-mail, and even open office doors can invite unwanted interruptions. It's not just the time that the interruption takes, but more significant than that is the time it takes to get your mind back to a focused productive state. There is an incredible amount of time and productivity lost in the, "Now, where was I?" state. Follow the guides in this book and eliminate anything that is likely to pull your attention away from the task at hand.

- **Keep sticky notes handy.** By placing a pad nearby, but out of your field of vision, you give yourself an outlet for any thoughts or ideas that might come to you. For instance, if you're working on a quarterly report, and you remember that you need to make an important call later, simply jot it down. You can review the note later, and the act of writing it should clear it from your mind.

The cost of interruptions to the U.S. economy is estimated at $588 billion a year. —Jonathan B. Spira, *The Cost of Not Paying Attention*, Basex Research, 2005

Live by the **moment;** after all, **life** is a series of moments.

—Trent Woodard

Tip 5

Decide Now

The biggest reason we have counters and desks that are piled high is because we wait to make decisions. We fill our counter with mail we think we might get back to. We put stuff on the table that we plan on getting back to. I know of someone who fills the counter, when that is full, he cleans it off by putting it in the closet. When the closet is full, it all goes to the basement. Needless to say, his basement is full of piles and junk that he will likely never get to because of indecision.

Simply put, you can "decide now" in order to enjoy less stress and greater clarity and productivity.

Here's how to start:

- Think. When you are about to put something down, really think: Is this where it goes? Am I really going to get back to this? Will I just need to throw this out later? Will I deal with this in less than a week?

- **Take time now.** Write the thank-you note now rather than putting down on a sticky note to write one later. Read the article now rather than waiting for the perfect 15 minute break that you never get. If at all possible do it, use it, throw it, or complete it now. You are likely not coming back to it.

Clutter is a result
of delayed decisions.

—Audrey Thomas

Indecision is the thief of opportunity.

—Jim Rohn

Tip 6

SEEDS First

Seeds grow best when the soil is cultivated, watered, and fertilized. People grow the most when they are ready physically, mentally, and spiritually. It is hard to accomplish a big goal if you are sick and tired. In order to be most effective as a person you need to make sure you plant your SEEDS first. My wife, Lisa, inspired this strategy and our family seeks to live by it daily. Before we tackle big projects, we make an effort to tend to our SEEDS.

S = Sleep. If you are tired all the time, you cannot do your best work, making that big goal nearly impossible to reach.

E = Exercise. As the saying goes, "pay now or pay later." A lack of exercise results in poor health, lack of focus, and lethargy. When I started exercising regularly, I felt so much better that my attitude and focus more than paid back the time I spent at the gym.

E = Eat right. For me, eating right includes:

- eating four vegetables a day
- limiting sugar, low-value carbohydrates, and fats
- avoiding processed meats and drinks that contain calories

D = Drink Water. When I drink 8-12 glasses of water a day, I feel better and crave bad foods less.

S = Source. For Lisa and me, our ultimate source is God. When we look to God for direction and give Him our gratitude, we find the strength, energy, and focus to accomplish our tasks, big and small.

> Before tackling a big goal, take care of your SEEDS:
> - **S**leep
> - **E**xercise
> - **E**at right
> - **D**rink water
> - **S**ource of strength

A healthy body is a guest-chamber for the soul;
a sick body is a prison. —Francis Bacon

Quality means doing it **right** when *no one* is looking.

—Henry Ford

Tip 7

Manage Your Energy

Understanding yourself can boost your productivity significantly. The key is completing the right tasks at the right time. When do you feel at your best? We all have a time of day when we feel most creative and productive. While a few people are more alert and energized in the afternoon or evening, most of us are charged up in the morning.

With that in mind, how do we spend these hours? Is it working on the projects and activities that require the most effort? Sadly, the answer is usually "no." We stumble into work and burn the best part of our day checking e-mail, reading the newspaper, and catching up with coworkers. We throw away the chance to do our best work for an extra cup of coffee, and then we wonder where the day went.

To fight this tendency, think about what your perfect day would be like. I don't mean some fantasy, but your ideal eight or nine hours of work—a day when you would be ultra productive. What would you get done and when? How would you match your most challenging tasks to your natural moods and energy level?

The next step, of course, is to begin managing your workload to match your peak productivity times. For example, I feel my best early on, so I arrange my day to complete creative tasks in the morning. I use my afternoons for activities that either don't require a great deal of mental energy, like paperwork, or those that energize me by allowing me to interact with others, such as phone calls and meetings. I am an extrovert, so this suits me very well.

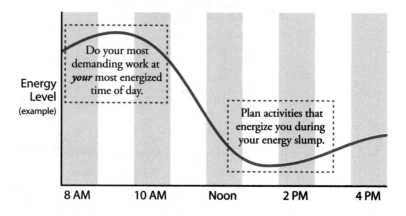

By working with my natural rhythms, instead of against them, I'm able to accomplish more in a shorter period of time. You can do the same. Simply pay attention to when you feel best and work around that.

A 10-year study of busy managers in nearly a dozen large companies showed that fully 90% of managers squander their time in all sorts of ineffective activities. In other words, a mere 10% of managers spend their time in a committed, purposeful, and reflective manner. —Dr. Helke Bruch and Dr. Sumantra Ghoshal, Harvard Business Review, 2/2002

I have always been
delighted
at the prospect of
a new day,
a fresh try, one more start,
with perhaps
a bit of magic
waiting somewhere
behind the morning.

—J.B. Priestly

Log It

Go to see any financial advisor in the country, and they'll likely advise you to keep track of everything you spend for a week or two. The reason for this is that most of us don't clearly know where our money is going. That is, beyond the mortgage and car payments, we usually stay blissfully unconscious of our more minor spending habits.

That would be fine, except that those minor habits add up. The four-dollar latte, purchased each morning, ends up costing nearly fifteen hundred dollars a year. Add in other impulsive buys, and it's easy to understand how little purchases can build into huge sums.

The way you spend your time is the same way. Your day probably consists of some big items as well as lots of smaller ones. And you might be surprised to know what they add up to. So, as a starting point to making yourself more efficient and productive, keep a time log for a week.

Here's how to make it work:

- **Commit to it.** Almost everyone resists the idea of keeping a time log, even though they're always amazed at the results afterwards. The information you get from logging your minutes will open your eyes and change the way you spend your time.

- **Write it down.** From phone calls to coffee breaks, make a note of the minute you start doing something and when you stop. Be as accurate as possible and don't cheat. The clearer the picture, the more beneficial it will be.

TIME LOG	
DATE	
TIME	ACTIVITY
8:00 AM	
8:15 AM	
8:30 AM	
8:45 AM	
9:00 AM	

- **See results.** When your week has ended, take a look at the totals. Which activities took the most time? Was it what you expected? Lots of people discover that they spent far longer than they imagined on things like socializing, reading newspapers, and surfing the internet. The good news is, they can take that information, be more conscious of their time, and ultimately make a bigger impact.

I know from experience that many of you will be tempted to skip over this exercise, but I encourage you to give it a try. Without accurate information, you won't be able to make appropriate adjustments.

On a typical day, office workers are interrupted about seven times an hour, which adds up to 56 interruptions a day, 80% of which are considered trivial, according to time-management experts.

—Wendy Cole, TIME Magazine, 10/11/2004

We are what we
repeatedly do.
Excellence,
then, is not an act,
but a habit.

— Aristotle

Tip 9

Excellence,
Not Perfection

Excellence is efficient; perfectionism is not. At some point, you have to stop. I have seen many perfectionist business people get very little done.

This is not an endorsement for careless work. I strive for excellence and seek to provide outstanding service to my clients. I spend a great deal of time and resources on my speeches, consulting, and books, and value the importance of putting excellence into everything that I do. Part of achieving excellence is doing great work. Another part is doing it on time. The problem with perfectionists is that they often miss deadlines because they don't finish their task.

These are a few techniques for delivering excellent work without giving in to perfectionism:

- **Do it right the first time.** When you are working on something, give it your full concentration. Put your all into the task at hand. Chances are, you will do a great job and won't need to come back to it later.

- **Give yourself a time limit.** Estimate how long it should take you to do something well, and then stick to it. Once you have made the decision to move on to the next step at a certain time, you may find that you were more efficient in completing the task.
- **Know when to stop.** You have to know when a project is finished. At a certain point, more changes are not making things better; they are just making them different. Learn to finish your work, check it over, and then move on to the next thing.
- **Get feedback.** If you aren't sure whether you are bettering your work or not, get feedback from a colleague or supervisor. An outside perspective can help you overcome perfectionist tendencies.

Done is better than perfect. —Mark LeBlanc

Great results speak infinitely louder than perfect ideas.

Plan Tomorrow Today

Though an old idea, this is one of the most valuable. It's hard to get a running start on the day without a plan. An old aphorism says, "He who fails to plan, plans to fail." You don't want to waste your creative morning time wondering what you should do today. If you want to attack your day, instead of have it attack you, here is a simple solid strategy.

Take the last 15 minutes of a workday to plan and prioritize the activities for the next day. This will set you up for success and also keep you from forgetting about important tasks or appointments.

Here are a couple strategies to help you out:

- **Prioritize your to-do list.** Count the items on your to-do list, and then number them in order from most important to least. For instance, if you have seven things to do, then the most important—probably one of your DMA's (see *Tip 2*)—gets a number seven. The next most important gets a six, and so on.

- **Repeat the process, in order of urgency.** That is, figure out what must be done soonest and give it a seven, what is second most urgent gets a six, etc. When you've finished, all you have to do is add the two numbers together. *Those with the highest combined scores are to be done first,* and on down through the list. By going through this simple process, you ensure that you're spending your time on what matters most.

Example:

To-Do Item	Importance	Urgency	TOTAL
Finish tax report	7	7	14
Send Packets to Speaker's Bureau	4	6	10
Write Trust Temp Article	2	4	6
Call Mark	6	2	8
Approve manuscript	3	5	8
Update Trust Temp 360 Web Header	1	3	4
Lunch with Joe?	5	1	6

- **Put it on paper.** Without being overly detailed, write down your schedule for the day. Having your activities on paper will keep you on track toward finishing your work for the day, and crossing finished items off can be very satisfying.

Every minute you spend planning saves you
an average of approximately 10 minutes
in execution. —Brian Tracy, Eat That Frog

You only live once, but if you work it right, *once is enough.*

—Joe E. Lewis

Tip 11

Energize

If you aren't excited about what you do, your lack of enthusiasm is going to slow you down.

Don't believe me? Think about the last time you walked into a fast food restaurant or a gas station and encountered someone who wasn't remotely satisfied with their job. How quickly were they moving? Excited people move faster, and with more purpose, while those who are bored or disengaged do not.

Here are a few ways to get fired up:

- **Think of the bigger picture.** Catch the big vision of what your work is really about. If you are a road construction worker, then you give people freedom, security, and safety. I recently met a machinist who makes tiny metal parts. He is both excited and motivated to do well because he understands that his tiny metal parts go into heart monitors that save lives! Envision the difference you are making to your family, your employer, and you will be motivated to do good work.

- **Act it.** By acting excited, you can trick your mind into feeling that way. When you feel a lack of enthusiasm, try putting on a smile and see if your mood catches up.

- **Move on.** If you can't find a way to be excited about what you are doing, that's probably a sure sign that you need to move on. Tough days come in any job, but if you've lost the passion for your work, then it may be time to make a tough decision.

- **Celebrate little things.** Keep saying things like, "That was great!" "Can't wait to see…" or "Thanks for getting that done." Even a tiny glimpse of excitement is contagious and helps bring other people up. Someone said we're all like people dog-paddling to stay above the water. Everything we say can either help someone stay afloat or make them sink further. Get excited and share that, because excitement keeps people going.

U.S. companies lose between $200-$300 billion a year due to absenteeism, tardiness, burnout, decreased productivity, worker's compensation claims, increased employee turnover, and medical insurance costs resulting from employee work-related stress.

—National Safety Council, Priority Magazine, 1/2/07

Where the heart
is **willing**,
it will find
a thousand ways.

Where it
is **unwilling**,
it will find
a thousand excuses.

—Arlen Price

Tip 12

Go Ready

1111

Would you knowingly board a flight if you knew the pilot hadn't slept in days? I'm willing to bet you wouldn't. We all recognize the importance of having that person in the cockpit awake and alert. More than that, we expect them to be prepared for the job at hand by arming themselves with things like maps, flight plans, and weather reports. We expect them to show up ready to work and regard anything else as completely unacceptable and dangerous.

Why don't we apply the same standards to ourselves? Walk into any office, first thing in the morning, and you're bound to find a number of people who are physically present, but clearly are not ready to do their jobs. Some of them are too sleepy to concentrate; others are still dwelling on problems or situations at home; and still more are intent on talking about what they saw on television than they are on getting anything done.

But no matter what the underlying symptom is, they all stem from a common cause—not feeling ready to work. Showing up unprepared is a bad habit, and one that could be costing you time and money. Here's how to break it:

- **Do SEEDS first.** See Tip #6 on taking care of yourself physically, mentally, and spiritually.

- **Be true.** You are paid to work. You are paid to deliver results. Have the integrity to come to work ready to deliver, not just talk about current events and the latest TV show. The office is not the place to dwell on arguments or to make dinner reservations.

- **Be ready anywhere.** In your briefcase or bag, stash some reading material you've been meaning to catch up on. This could be an industry journal, a report, or even a career development book. One of my best friends always has a good book with him—that way he is less stressed and doesn't feel like he is wasting time if he has to wait for someone.

- **Don't forget your notebook.** Take advantage of time away from the office by carrying a small notebook for brainstorming or mind mapping. Creative thinking can happen in the most unexpected moments.

Employees spend an average of 36 minutes per day at work on personal tasks. By gender, men take 44 minutes and women 29 minutes, with the 18-34 year old group using the most time.

—Office Team Surveys, February 2007

What you have to do and
the way you have to do it
is incredibly simple.

Whether you are
willing to do it,
that's another matter.

—Peter F. Drucker

Efficient E-mail

E-mail is a lot like a medication—it can cure a lot of things, but you have to be careful of the side effects. E-mail can be used as an effective form of communication, or it can be a costly interrupter. Before you count yourself out of this suggestion, try implementing the following ideas:

1. **Close your e-mail.** With your e-mail minimized on your computer screen, you can be visually interrupted by popup notifications and audibly interrupted by chimes or other sounds that may occur. That constant interruption takes you away from focusing and being productive. Maybe you can check all e-mails that collect in the inbox at morning, noon, and late in the day or at the most at the top of every hour. Just make sure it is when you choose and when several have collected instead of being interrupted for each one separately.

2. **Get to ten or less e-mails in your inbox.** It's easy to get caught up in mounting lists of e-mails in your inbox. Two things can happen. First, you spend an exorbitant amount of time reading new e-mails and sifting through old ones. Secondly, you could be

overwhelmed and do nothing. Important e-mails could be lost in the abyss. When you have ten or fewer e-mails in your Inbox, it feels great and productivity and clarity increase.

To get to ten or less e-mails in your inbox, take a day to catch up and then do the following *every time you open an e-mail.* Every message you get should be handled in one of four ways:

- **Delete or archive it.** If no follow up is required, get rid of it.

- **Deal with it.** Sometimes all that's needed is a quick confirmation or other response. If you can answer in two minutes or less, do it right away.

- **File it.** Learn to use your folders and subfolders to archive messages you don't need now, but might want to keep for the future.

- **Flag it for follow up or attach it to your calendar.** If a message needs action, but you aren't ready to deal with it yet, use your program's alert or flag function. The reminder will bring it back when you need it, but in the meantime it will be off of your mind.

3. **Only use e-mail for information sharing.** E-mail is not for emotional messages. If you need to correct someone or fire them, pick up the phone or meet in person. Even encouragement is better delivered through a written note or face-to-face communication. Stop and think: "Is e-mail the best channel for this communication?"

A recent study from the University of London concluded that your IQ falls 10 points when you're taking constant calls, e-mails and text messages—the same amount as if you'd lost an entire night's sleep, or more than double the loss that came with smoking marijuana.

It's not enough
to be busy.
The question is:
What are we
busy about?
—Henry David Thoreau

Tip 14

Phone Habits

Like e-mail, the phone is a wonderful tool for communicating quickly, as long as it is used correctly. You only get 24 hours each day, so try not to burn too many of them talking to telemarketers or chatting about the weather.

Here are a few more ways to use the phone effectively:

- **Make a plan.** Before you dial, take a moment to think about what you want to say. Are there any major points to be covered or questions to be resolved? Write them down on a sticky note or a slip of paper. You can lose a lot of time with excessive follow-up calls.

- **Get to the point.** If you are really serious about cutting down your phone time, or need to be encouraged to get to the point more quickly, buy a small kitchen timer and place it next to your phone. Every time you make or receive a call, start it. Few things remind you to get to the point faster than seeing the minutes and seconds count down right in front of you. Plus, while people like and need friendliness, getting to the point shows respect.

- **Screen.** Not everyone who rings you has something important to say, especially if you're working on a critical project. Get in the habit of making appointments for important calls.

- **Make voice mails brief.** Never leave long rambling messages. Instead, think for a moment about what you need to convey and then deliver it succinctly. Be sure to indicate whether you need the other person to return your call, the best time for them to call back, and always speak slowly and clearly when leaving your phone number. I am still getting better at this, but I sure appreciate those who do it well.

- **Be present.** If at all possible, turn off your phone during meetings. Don't answer calls and stop texting. I know someone who lost a $500 million deal because he took a call during an important lunch meeting. In many cases, if everyone would avoid interruptions during meetings, they would last half as long!

A poll conducted for Staples found that almost half of the small-business managers in the United States work during time meant for family, while 49 percent make business calls and check e-mail messages while behind the wheel; 18 percent read e-mail messages in the bathroom.

Habit and routine
have an unbelievable
power to
waste and destroy.
—Henri De Lubac

Maximize
Meetings

ᑖᑐ᥎᥎᥎᥎ᑖ

Long, pointless meetings—a major complaint across every single
industry—are among the worst in business habits because they
kill productivity two ways: they waste time and kill morale. Instead
of getting important work done, entire offices are packed into rooms,
often for no good reason.

It would be silly to suggest we can do away with meetings altogether.
After all, it's the synergy created from combining our thoughts and
ideas that allows most projects to succeed. We just need to go about
them efficiently; otherwise, they can be a drag on everyone's time and
energy.

Here are some techniques to make your meetings shorter and more
worthwhile:

- **Hold fewer meetings.** Lots of meetings are unnecessary.
  Eliminate the unproductive ones from your calendar.

- **Start them off on the right foot.** If you are leading or chairing the meeting, be clear about what you want to accomplish. The clearer your vision or mission for the time, the more likely you are to achieve it.

- **Set shorter agendas.** Meetings tend to fill available time. So, if you set aside an hour to go over a new initiative, it's likely to take at least that long. On the other hand, if you make it clear that you only expect things to go on for 15 minutes, there's a much greater chance you will get to the point faster.

- **Schedule them back to back.** By having another meeting to go to, you give yourself (and any other parties) a deadline to wrap things up.

- **Go public.** Coffee shops and other public locales can make for great places to meet because you're less likely to be interrupted by your staff, the office phone, or other distractions you might have in your workspace. Just be sure the time you spend getting away doesn't outweigh the minutes saved.

On an average day, there are 17 million meetings in America.

—Donald Whetmore, Productivity Institute

The one
who claims that
it cannot be done
should not interrupt
the one
who is doing it.

—unknown

Tip 16

Flight Plan

D o you travel for work? Getting anywhere takes some time. Even a domestic flight can take several hours, and that's without factoring in delays and missed connections. You have a choice to make with that time—it can either be lost to games and newspapers, or used to be productive. Why waste it?

Get the most out of your time by composing a flight plan:

- **Write it down.** Like DMA's (see *Tip 2*), I simply write my flight plan down on a sticky note. I list the most important things I can do while at the airport and in flight.

- **Come prepared to work.** Make sure to pack any files or documents you will need in a carry-on bag or briefcase. And remember to have the computer battery charged for the flight.

- **Expect the unexpected.** The modern hub and spoke system that airlines use means that more passengers can get more places in the world, most of the time. But it also means that thunderstorms in Zurich can leave you stranded in Kansas City. Always bring along something you can work on if you find yourself with an unexpected block of free time.

- **Bring backup.** Extra cords, batteries, pens, and other supplies are essential. Without them, you might find yourself packing up or powering down in the middle of a project.
- **Anticipate your energy level.** An outbound flight to a major conference is a great time to fine-tune your presentation. A return flight of a ten-day road trip is not. Recognize that there will be times when you aren't going to be up to doing your best work. If you know you're going to be tired, do something simple like light reading.

Finally, for any travel, ask yourself one question—how important is this trip? If your objectives can be accomplished via phone or e-mail, or if it's more efficient for the other party to come to you, skip the journey altogether. Traveling takes a lot of time, and so does recovering from days away from home and the office. Only take to the skies when you are sure it's necessary.

In 2007, flight delays
added up to 170 years of lost time.

—Washington Post

It's the constant and
determined effort
that breaks down *resistance*,
sweeps away all obstacles.

—Claude M. Bristo

Tip 17

Wake Up

ʔ1111ʕ

Years ago, there was a commercial for the armed forces in which young men and women were seen running through obstacle courses, guiding jets, and otherwise keeping the free world safe. Each ad would end by reminding prospective recruits that those in the military "did more before breakfast than most people did all day."

Not only is this a catchy slogan, it holds some truth. A vast number of the world's highest achievers, in nearly every field, credit their success to "showing up early." The most effective people I have worked with have been early risers.

A friend's grandma often said, "You get twice as much done in the morning than in the afternoon." I am not sure why it is so true, but it is. By getting up earlier, not only can you get more done, but you will probably miss much of the traffic and congestion that comes from getting to work when everyone else does.

Here are a few ways to get started:

- **Conquer the snooze button.** If you have a tendency to keep pressing it, you might have to take drastic action. In most cases, moving your alarm away from your bed or turning it to a very high volume will do the trick.

- **Get enough sleep.** Getting up early doesn't have to mean missing out on sleep. Many people stay up much later than they intend to watching TV shows or spending time on other mindless fillers, when they could be getting rejuvenating rest. Try trading an hour at night for one in the morning; it might change your life.

- **Use the extra time wisely.** I like to start my day with a bit of exercise and then accomplish my DMA's (see *Tip 2*). Doing so gives me momentum for the rest of the morning and afternoon.

58% of American workers take care of
their most important business in the morning
and 47% take care of it during mid-morning.

— www.daytimer.com

With each sunrise,
we start anew.

—Anonymous

Tip 18

Clear Desk

A clear desk leads to a clear mind, which leads to high productivity and laser focus. When you look at your workspace, what do you see? Is it clear and organized, prompting you to begin your most important tasks? Or is it cramped and cluttered, overflowing with printed reports, unopened mail, an array of sticky notes, and other distractions? The answer might be a strong indicator for how much you get done.

Many people have come to think of a disorganized area as the sign of a busy person who is getting lots of things done. The truth, however, is that a messy desk invites your mind to wander. No matter what you are doing, your attention is subconsciously pulled this way and that, wondering "what should I do with that thing…" and "when will I get to those?" Clean desks, on the other hand, lead to productivity and concentration by encouraging you to finish whatever you're working on at the moment.

Here's how to keep your desk distraction-free:

- **Touch everything once.** Dealing with the same file or piece of mail repeatedly is a waste of time. When something arrives to your desk, decide whether to file it, act on it, or throw it away the first time.

- **Clean up your office.** Naturally, it's easier to keep your desk clean if your office isn't overflowing with unaddressed paperwork or other distractions. Devote a few minutes each day to keeping your space orderly.

- **Keep a tickler file.** A tickler file is where you put paper you need to take action on in the future. To set up this system, follow these steps:

  1. Clear out one of your file desk drawers.

  2. Put in one hanging file folder labeled for each month of the year. Then label manila folders 1-31 to represent the possible days in a month. Put these 31 manila folders inside the current month's hanging folder.

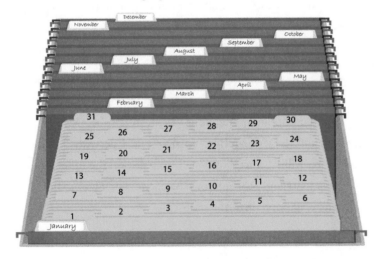

3. Now, file everything on your desk into the day or month that you want to deal with it. Each day, move that day's empty folder to the next month's hanging file. When you get to the end of a month, move that hanging folder to the back of the file, where it now functions as the following year.

> *For example, if it were March 15th you would have March's hanging folder in the front of your file with manila folder days 15-31 in order inside of it. Days 1-14 would be inside April's hanging folder directly behind March. When you get to the office, you pull out the manila folder numbered 15 and find exactly what you have to do that day then place that folder in order behind folder number 14 in April.*

Build your tickler system in a way that works best for your particular needs. Some people find it simpler to have a manila folder for each week instead of each day. Some might find it necessary to have two months' of numbered manila day folders. Some fill in next month's day folders as they go. Some would rather collect everything for the next month and a few days before the new month starts, they file the month into the daily folders they desire. Perhaps you'd like to take this idea, but make it digital instead. The point is that you adapt these ideas until you find what works for you.

The great time-saver is this: If you discover a task that doesn't need to be addressed until a later date, then put it in the day or month you want to take action on it. You don't have to think about it or try to remember to do it—it will pop up exactly when you want it to. Another benefit is the ability to look at the next few days and re-file or deal with urgent matters should you need to clear your schedule for a few days.

To keep your desk perfectly clear, you may need to add a few additional hanging files. I have extra files behind my tickler months for receipts, things to read, and things to file. "Things to file" holds papers I file in other filing systems at the end of each month. "Things to read" allows me a place to throw magazines and items I can pull out when I know I'll be sitting in the airport with extra time. If keeping digital files of reference reading material is more up your alley, check out the application called Instapaper.

A messy desk or office isn't the sign of a busy professional; it's the sign of a disorganized one. Make it clear to yourself and others that you want to concentrate and work hard by keeping your space organized for that purpose.

Rifling though messy desks
wastes 1.5 hours a day. —AOL

You either
get organized
or you
get crushed.

—Donald J. Trump

Automate

You've heard the old saying, "Don't reinvent the wheel." I like it, partly because it is catchy, and partly because it is shorter than, "Create templates and systems so you don't have to duplicate the repetitive tasks in your work." Don't you agree?

Either one is getting at the same concept. E-mails, reports, newsletters and other material, when created from scratch, usually represents time lost. A much better strategy is to keep a file of the items you will use over and over and simply fill in the blanks each time you need one. It will save you time, and probably allow for more complete, well-prepared information.

For instance, suppose you know a question that the majority of your clients and customers will eventually ask about your products. Rather than answer it each time over the phone or e-mail, why not write out one thorough answer and keep it as a document that you can e-mail out whenever you need? By simply adding a new name, and possibly a couple of details, you can send out a well-reasoned and individualized answer in seconds.

Here's how to make automation work:

- **Search through your correspondence.** Are there questions or issues that pop up again and again? As a general rule of thumb, if you answer something more than once a week, you could benefit from using a template.

- **Be thorough.** Since your goal is to make a template to use repeatedly, make it as thorough and complete as possible. If you notice follow-up questions or input from others, be sure to amend them.

- **Make them easy to customize.** One trick I use is to leave information that needs to be filled in the template as bold or all caps. For example, markers like NAME or address make it easy for me to remember to fill that info in before I send anything out.

- **Keep them front and center.** Your computer desktop is a good place for your boilerplate answers and info. Wherever you save the file, make it simple to return to that place.

The proper use of macros can save the average office more than 10 hours per week. —Microsoft

---

Try again.
Fail again.
Fail better.
—Samuel Beckett

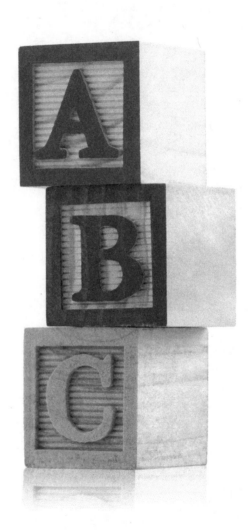

Tip 20

To-do List
ABC's

W hether you use a paper or electronic to-do list (I like Microsoft Notebook Layout), it helps to know the to-do list ABC's.

My notebook is divided into four categories. The first are DMA's (see *Tip 2*) which are actually written on a sticky note. Since I like to do these during my quiet hour, first thing in the morning, they are the first to be completed and crossed off. From there, I just do my ABC's:

- A items = things you have to do today because they are important tasks. Items get crossed off as I accomplish each one. If there is time, I scan the B list for the most important items and start on those.

- B items = things to do soon, but not necessarily today. These tasks are important, but not urgent. For example, my passport is about to expire. Because I'm scheduled for an upcoming international trip, I need to renew it soon, although I might not get to it today.

- C items = things that you want to do sometime, but that are not urgent or overly important now. For instance, I might want to learn a new skill, take another speed-reading course, or buy an office building. I want to prioritize them sometime, but maybe not this month or even this year. By keeping them in my notebook, I'm reminded of them from time to time without having them occupy my mental energy.

Good things happen when
you get your priorities straight.

—Scott Caan

The secret
of getting ahead
is getting
started.

—Mark Twain

Tip 21

Master
Faster

⌒⌒⌒⌒
ꓶꓶꓶꓶ

In business and life, there is a tendency to overlook the obvious. This might not apply anywhere else as strongly as it does to productivity. Lost in the collections of tips and techniques is one of the most straightforward ways to get more out of your day—do things faster.

Many may groan and think, "We're working as hard and as fast as we can." But the truth is that they're working as hard and as fast as they *know how*. Executives may feel as though members of their support team are not working efficiently. Let's look at this issue from an individual perspective as well as from a team perspective. You might find room for improvement in both!

There are methods and techniques for everyday tasks that would save precious time. Perhaps someone on your staff needs a speed reading class or advanced typing practice. The average office employee could save several hours a week by learning to do their common tasks faster.

Creating a clear workspace changed my productivity dramatically, but it wasn't until I understood the value of doing things faster, that I gained a significant increase in productivity. I have also learned to communicate with my team about the delicate balance between work quality and efficiency. It has changed my thought process when hiring for certain positions as well.

Here are some tips for doing things faster:

- **Scope out topics.** Speed reading, typing, computer shortcuts, systemizing techniques, and research skills are a few areas any businessperson could benefit from studying. There are probably dozens of others in your industry. To find them, research topics online or better yet, find a successful colleague who excels in this area and ask him or her for ideas.

- **Find classes.** Cities large and small have community colleges and education programs offering low-cost evening classes on certain computer programs, speed reading, and so on. Announcement boards, local papers, and online schools are other great places to find beneficial classes. Offering to pay for your admin to take certain classes could benefit the company as well as help improve his or her skill set for the future.

- **Hire it done.** You might get things done faster if you hire part of it out. Maybe you need to know more about a new technology but don't have time to do the research. Hire someone from a website like guru.com or elance.com to do the research for your review. Or consider an additional admin for your office or team. Assign tasks to each admin according to their skills. Perhaps one is gifted at greeting clients and talking with them on the phone while the other is very efficient at making travel plans or creating documents when he or she is able to work without interruption.

- **Find a mentor.** Maybe you have a friend who has found a successful morning routine at the office, or maybe you have a colleague who has streamlined the same task that you need to do on a regular basis. Ask for help. I have found that people are honored, not offended by such questions.

- **Be self-taught.** Many skills can be learned in a few minutes a day without any kind of formal training. Simply find a popular book on the subject and follow the exercises.

By learning to do something twice as fast, you make it possible to do twice as much. So keep sharpening your skills and you will find you're giving yourself the gift of several extra hours each week.

The average American reads approximately 250 words per minute. With a few weeks' training, that will improve to more than 400 words per minute. —University of Victoria

---

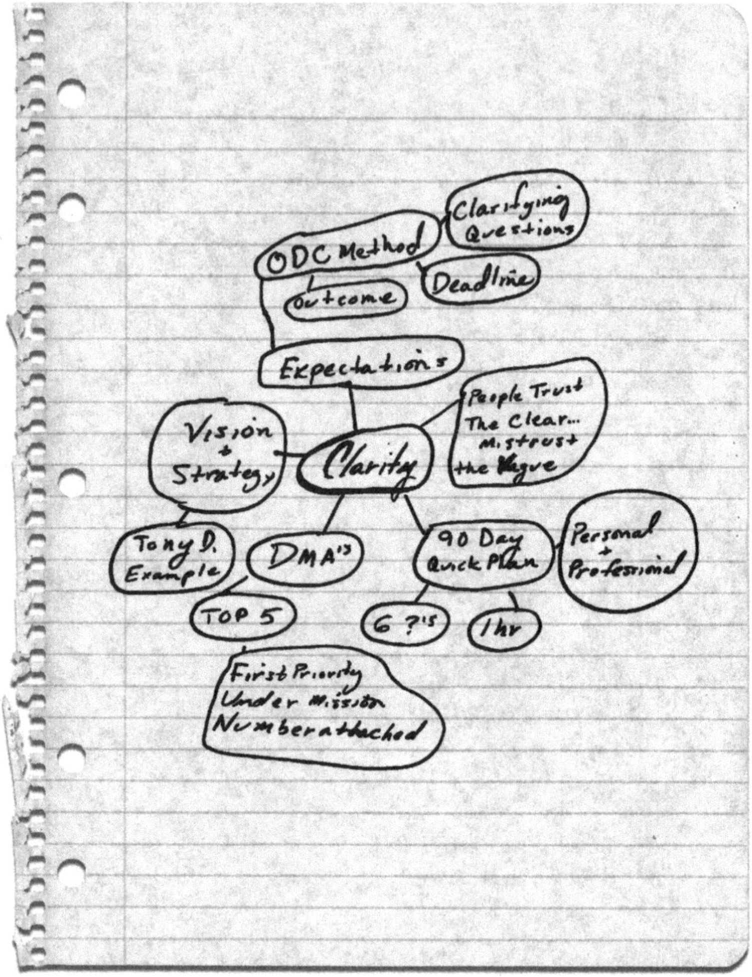
ODC Method
Clarifying Questions
Deadline
Outcome
Expectations
People Trust The Clear... Mistrust the Vague
Vision + Strategy
Clarity
Tony D. Example
DMA's
90 Day Quick Plan
Personal + Professional
TOP 5
6 ?'s
1hr
First Priority
Under Mission
Number attached

Tip 22

Mind
Mapping

One great way to cut through confusion and speed up organization is by mind mapping, a technique that encourages the free-flow thinking and creativity of all-out brainstorming, but yet organizes more effectively and efficiently so you can actually use it and save time. Designed to go beyond conventional note taking, it allows you to register ideas and concerns in relation to one another, rather than in list form. Mind Mapping has cut my presentation preparation time and book writing preparation time by a third. Learn this method and get ready to shave significant time off of planning and preparing for anything.

I've supplied a sample mind map on the facing page, but here are a few steps to get you started:

- **Begin in the middle of your paper.** Write down the question or issue that's on your mind, and then draw a circle around it.

- **Branch out.** With the topic established, draw some branches relating to major thoughts. For a simple example, if you were trying to decide on a restaurant for dinner, your branches might include cost, location, reviews, and wait time.

- **Stick with brief concepts.** Since you want to get your thoughts down quickly and succinctly, short ideas and phrases are best. Abbreviations are fine, as long as you remember what they stand for.

- **Look both ways.** In most cases, your map will start with a central idea and branch out, but feel free to make any other connections that exist.

- **Mix pictures with words.** Don't be afraid to use drawings, colors, graphs, or any other tools that will make your map more vivid. The point is to use your mind, not stick to rules.

- **Go deeper.** Say you want to write an article on leadership but that is too big of a topic. Your first map may have integrity, vision, strategy, and courage around it. You could then go deeper and do a map on integrity, which would point to account-ability, character, congruence etc. You can go deep on each of these points that would be in your article called "Integrity in Leadership."

95% of self-improvement books, audio tapes, and video tapes purchased are not used.

—Donald Whetmore Productivity Institute

The **mind** can be trained to relieve itself on **paper.**

—Poet Billy Collins

Tip 23

Back Up

ꝏ 1111 ꝏ

O ne of the biggest time-wasters, in any business, is dealing with crises that could have been anticipated. Computer failures are the prime example of what I mean. We need our laptops and tablets to do our work and run our businesses, but they're predictably unreliable.

Here are some tips for making a dropped notebook or a crashed hard drive into a minor inconvenience instead of a major-league headache:

- **Set up a system.** Make sure your critical files are being backed up on a regular basis. Otherwise, you could lose months or more of work, client data, and personal information in the blink of an eye.

- **Use it regularly.** There are several programs that will allow you to automate your backups, updating themselves daily, weekly, or monthly. It doesn't matter when you do it, so long as it happens at regular intervals. Some back-up companies to check out include www.carbonite.com and www.mozy.com.

- **Store backups separately.** If you are backing up your files on a hard drive, it's a good idea to keep your backups in a place away from your home or office. That way, you won't lose both in the event of fire, water damage, theft, or another catastrophe. For help with back-ups, networks, or related tech needs, check out www.cimbura.com.

Backing up your vital data only takes a few minutes, and it could save you days of effort if something happens to your hardware. If you have someone on your team taking care of these things, this might be a good time to check with them on what tools are being used to insure that your files are retrievable.

Notebooks bought in 2003 and 2004
had a failure rate of 20%, rising to 28%
by year four. —Gartner Studies

Prepare for the unknown by studying how others *in the past* **have coped with** the unforeseeable and the **unpredictable.**

—George S. Patton

Tip 24

Go Paperless

111

Paper files are incredibly inefficient. They're heavy, expensive to keep, and easily damaged. A better solution may be to go with a paperless office. I have not made the transition fully myself, but I have friends and associates who have, and I am moving in that direction. What a space and time saver!

For less than you would spend on a dinner out with your family, you can buy a scanner that can store countless data digitally. And best of all, it can be kept on your hard drive or the cloud, not in a cabinet or in piles. While there are many ways to go about making your office paperless, you might find the Evernote app and associated products (evernote.com) helpful. They have great tools for capturing those random thoughts and ideas that are so hard to keep track of on paper.

Here are a few tips for making a paperless office work for you:

- **Use keywords.** One of the handiest features of a digital file cabinet is that each document can be marked with a series of keywords, making them easier to search and find later. Make sure each scanned piece is noted with a few terms that apply most directly to the content.

- **Keep the file tree simple.** As with your inbox, you want to keep your files organized, but not complicated. Make sure that each document has a logical place so you can find it in a search.

- **Back up everything.** It goes without saying that you don't want a computer failure to wipe out all of your records. Get a good backup system and use it consistently.

- **Keep hard copies for a few weeks.** Important documents, like contracts, should be kept as hard copies for a few weeks, along with those that you use every day. Digital copies aren't more efficient if you need to pull them up every hour. You might find there are certain documents that need to be kept, but at least you have come a long way toward simplifying your work at the office.

The average North American uses
nearly 12,000 sheets of paper each year.
—UNESCO Statistical Handbook

What you
don't **know**
may not hurt you,
but what you
don't **remember**
always does.

—Gerald M. Weinberg

Tip 25

Shortcuts

Mouse clicks are to a productive person what body hair is to an Olympic swimmer—precious seconds that can be shaved off. Opening menus and selecting commands might not seem like a big deal, but it can add up to several moments wasted every time you use them.

To speed things up, get into the habit of using keyboard shortcuts. Every piece of software you use comes with them, and most are easy to remember, like *Ctrl* + *S* to save, and *Ctrl* + *Z* to undo.

Here are a few guidelines to get you started:

- **Make a list.** Think of the programs you use most often, along with the commands within them. Once you've identified ten or twenty things you do frequently, find the appropriate shortcut on the web or in your manual. Alternatively, you could hire an expert or consultant who can show you a number of shortcuts in a few hours' time.

- **Keep them close.** In the beginning, you will want to keep a chart or some sticky notes with the shortcuts you use most. Over time, they'll become second nature and you won't need the reminders anymore.

Remember, learning shortcuts might seem to slow you down for the first few days, but by mastering them you can save yourself minutes each week, and hours every month.

The average person today (1999) receives more information on a daily basis than the average person received in a lifetime in 1900. —Productivity Institute

---

There is a time
in the life of
every problem
when it is
big enough to see,
yet *small enough*
to solve.

—Mike Leavitt

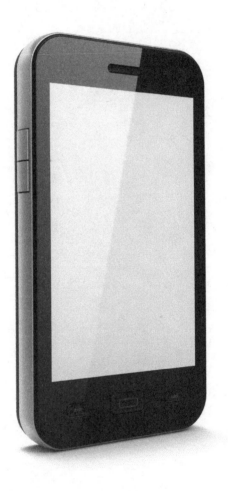

Tip 26

Don't
Go Gadget

I t would be easy to think, for all of their sleek advertising, that every mobile device and new app could solve any productivity problem. While they can do extraordinary things, the reality is that many of them end up costing more time and money than they save.

That doesn't mean that technology can't make our lives easier. It certainly can, as long as we're smart about integrating it:

- **Think.** Will this really help my productivity and make me more efficient and effective?

- **Be realistic.** Watch out for impulsive purchases! Don't fall for the trap. Before you commit to buying, look up information on the product and read reviews. Have someone on your team research the reviews for the product to be sure it is a good fit for your company. That way, you will have a realistic idea of what it can actually do for you, and whether it's worth the time and money.

- **Learn and know the features.** If you decide to buy the new electronic product, then take the time to figure out what it can do for you. You will get a lot more value out of your new purchase if you understand how it works.

31% of U.S. drivers ages 18-64 reported that they had read or sent text messages or e-mail messages while driving at least once within the 30 days before they were surveyed.

—Center for Disease Control and Prevention

Men have become
the tools
of their tools.

—Henry David Thoreau

Don't Get
Hooked

ᒍ 1 1 1 1 ᒧ

Ienjoy fishing. To catch a fish, I use a shiny hook called a lure. TV often lures people in and then hooks them before they know it. Countless studies have found that spending too much time with the television makes people more passive. Living life yourself is better than watching others. Just consider the following stats and quotes:

- 79% of adults believe Americans watch too much television, according to a Rasmussen Report.

- The value of Americans' time spent watching TV, assuming an average wage of only $5 per hour, is S1.25 trillion, according to California State University Northridge.

- Millions of Americans are so hooked on television that they fit the criteria for "substance abuse" as defined in the official psychiatric manual, according to Rutgers University psychologist, Robert Kubey.

- According to Dr. William H. Deitz, of Tufts University School of Medicine, "The easiest way to reduce inactivity is to turn off the TV set. Almost anything else uses more energy than watching TV."

- According to an American Journal of Public Health study, an adult who watches three hours of TV a day is far more likely to be obese than an adult who watches less than one hour. (Compiled by TV-Free America)

This principle extends further to include things like video games and web surfing. Your downtime should rejuvenate your body and mind.

None of this is to say that you shouldn't watch any television. But it is worth thinking through why, what, and when. So how do we break the spell of electronic time-wasters? Here are a few tips to get started:

- **Make it harder.** If TV really isn't that great for us, making it harder to watch may help replace the habit with a better one. My wife and I have made it harder by not buying cable and having only one TV in the house. No one goes off to their room to watch TV, and we find ourselves doing better things with our time.

- **Find other things to do.** The best way to cut down your TV time is to find a better alternative. Taking a new class, preparing a home-cooked dinner, or even playing a game of hoops are all great ways to forget about what's on TV and reenergize your mind and body.

- **Go to bed.** Many people watch late-night shows out of habit, when they'd be better served with another hour or two of sleep. If you often find yourself bleary-eyed in the morning, turn off the tube after dark and get some rest.

I find television
very educating.
Every time somebody
turns on the set,
I go into the other room
and read a book.
—Groucho Marx

Tip 28

Optimize

How many hours do you spend working on a computer each day? Many people spend half or more of their working hours in front of a screen. If too much of that time is spent waiting for your computer to start up and load programs, then you're wasting it needlessly.

Think of your computer a bit like a pack horse. It arrives young, fresh, and quick. But as it ages, and we pile more and more software on its back, it slows down. Eventually, it becomes so overloaded that it moves at a crawl no matter what you ask it to do. It might seem like a minor inconvenience, but consider this: if you spend ten minutes each day waiting for your machine to startup and programs to load, you've lost nearly an hour each week.

Here are a few ways to cut down on your computer's loading time and increase performance:

- **Work on one thing at a time.** Multitasking slows down machines in the same way it does people. Asking your computer to do too many things at once will lead to poor performance.

- **Periodically clean out clutter.** Old e-mails, file folders, and unused programs are like junk sitting around in your garage. Take some time, one Friday afternoon per month for example, and get rid of what you don't need.

- **Do maintenance on downtime.** Most computers will run optimization programs themselves—like disk defragmentation, backups, and so on—if you let them. These take time, so set them up to execute automatically overnight or through the weekend. It will leave your computer running faster, and won't take up your valuable productive hours.

- **Ask for help.** If you aren't an expert on computers, find someone who is. Rely on your team to help keep the computers in the office running efficiently. Even if your company doesn't have a designated IT department, you probably have a colleague, friend, or relative who can help you get things running smoothly.

According to efficiency experts,
the average computer user spends 9 minutes
every day waiting for files and web screens
to download. —Amazon

Luck is
what happens
when *preparation*
meets *opportunity*.

—Seneca

Tip 29

Bundle

Suppose you had to prepare a dozen cupcakes. Would you bake them one at a time? Of course not! And yet, that's exactly how some people approach their work. They make a couple of phone calls, write an e-mail, switch back to the phone, then work on a proposal, and so on. We've all succumbed to this counterproductive method. It forces your mind to switch gears more often than necessary and wastes time with each shift.

Luckily, this is one of the easiest tendencies to overcome. All it takes is a willingness to examine your daily workload and decide what tasks would be most efficiently accomplished together. Here are a few tips to get you started:

- **Start with the obvious.** Phone calls, e-mails, and paperwork are prime candidates to be grouped together. In most cases, they can be done more quickly and efficiently in a batch than one at a time. For changes specific to your work life, look through your calendar for other tasks that make sense to group together. Keep an eye toward saving time and staying focused, and you're bound to find at least a few.

- **Set a time limit.** Give yourself a deadline, thirty minutes for example, to finish the grouped jobs. This will keep you focused on getting through them without stalling or procrastinating. Consider designating a time period each day where you ask your team or admin for no interruptions. Your colleagues and team can help protect your time while you accomplish your tasks.

- **Stay in your seat.** When you start working on a group, decide that you will finish them before you get up to do anything else. It will help you concentrate and finish faster.

- **Have a "meeting day."** If possible, a great way to get through all of your meetings is to bundle them together. Having them back-to-back means it's easier to stay in the right mindset. And, you will have a good reason to keep each one to the point. If this is not feasible, an alternative would be to have a meeting-free day. Set aside one day in which you do not schedule or accept any meetings.

A study suggests that getting rid of
the gossip, jokes, and other unproductive e-mail
from colleagues can save up to 30 percent of the time
an employee spends reading e-mail. —Gartner Group

Efficiency is **intelligent** laziness.

—David Dunham

Tip 30

Get Un-stuck

Sometimes the sheer size or complexity of a project can leave us without a clear path forward. With so much to do and uncertainty about where to start, stress renders us paralyzed. In other words, we get stuck.

The good news, however, is that getting stuck doesn't have to mean staying stuck. Usually all it takes is a bit of progress to knock our minds loose and get us back on track. Here are a few tips for breaking out of mental gridlock:

- **Don't procrastinate.** The easiest thing in the world to do with a difficult job is to put it off. But this is nearly always guaranteed to make things tougher, not easier. Decide that you will work at one aspect of the problem, and don't give up until you've made some headway. In other words, do what needs to be done, whether you feel like it or not.

- **Start anywhere.** There is no rule saying you have to start a project in the beginning. If you are having trouble with the start, try attacking it from another angle. You might find that it frees up your mind and gets things moving.

- **Do small pieces.** If you are overwhelmed by the size of a task, break it down into the smallest pieces possible. For instance, a fifty-page report might consist of three sections, each of which has ten topics. Start with any one of those—your work will add up quickly.

- **Do something terrible.** Give yourself permission to do the job terribly at first. Without any pressure, you will probably get through it quickly and let go of enough anxiety to go back and do a better version on the second pass.

- **Use momentum.** Any of these techniques will help you get going. Once you've started, you will find it's much easier to keep the forward momentum.

After ten years of research on a project
that was only supposed to take five years,
a Canadian industrial psychologist found in a giant study
that not only is procrastination on the rise, it makes people
poorer, fatter and unhappier. —University of Calgary

Momentum
builds momentum.
—Stacy Stoldorf Guethling

Tip 31

Stock Up

Remember—anything that takes your mind or body away from the job at hand is making you less efficient and effective. Interruptions are the biggest enemy to productivity.

Take a peek in your desk drawers. What do you see? If the answer is, "whatever is needed to keep working, but nothing more," then you might not need to read this tip. But if it is anything else, you're probably losing time to distractions and unnecessary trips to the supply room.

With that in mind, it's important that you set up your workspace as much as possible with everything you will need to bring the task at hand from start to finish. Every time you're forced to get up for something—whether it's a fresh pen, more paper, or some background material, you lose the time it takes you to retrieve it as well as the time it takes to get your focus back.

Here's how to be sure you get sidetracked as little as possible:

- **Keep things stocked.** Most retail stores do an inventory once or twice a week to be sure they won't run out of merchandise. Put the same idea to work for you. Take a few minutes to be sure you have all the office supplies you need, in a place where you can find them. If you don't know where to find your supplies, then ask the right person on your team to help make sure those supplies are accessible to you and others who will need them. If your drawers are filled with things you don't need, clean them out. Let the items you need to work efficiently be visible and accessible to you.

- **Pack a couple of snacks.** Hunger is a big concentration killer. If you find you need frequent snack breaks, keep something healthy around to tide you over. A small bag of almonds or an apple can give you the boost you need to finish what you're doing.

- **Keep reference materials at your fingertips.** If your work requires you to frequently check a dictionary, medical manual, or any other reference book, keep a copy within arm's reach. If your searches are primarily done on the internet, consider getting a larger monitor or a second monitor so you can have several windows open at once. Some find the ipad is a good secondary tool for doing quick internet searches.

One-third of workers say they have
played computer games during work hours.
—Society of Financial Service Professionals

The **time** to
repair the roof
is when
the sun is **shining**.

—John F. Kennedy

Tip 32

Say No

There are millions of people out there who are overwhelmed because of one simple fact: They don't know how to say "no." I have been one of them. While volunteering is noble, and creating an indispensable role for yourself is good, not knowing when to say "no" leads to stress and often the inability to deliver on promises. Inability to say "no" can have you doing many good things without doing any of the greatest things.

Since we only have so much time and energy to give, here are a few strategies for cutting back:

- **Say Yes to the best and No to the rest.** It's not about declining all the jobs you dislike; it's about setting the right priorities. Sometimes, by saying no to one thing, you're freeing yourself to say yes to something better. Every choice is a sacrifice. When I choose to work, I am not with my family. When I am with my family, I'm not at work. Keep saying "yes" to the best things.

- **Budget your time wisely.** When you're asked to take on a new project or task, be as realistic as possible when estimating how long it will take. Think through the details, people, and processes involved before making a commitment, so you are sure to deliver.

- **Quick polite explanations are best.** If you're too busy to help or a given opportunity is not the best fit, all that's needed is a polite decline. By going into long explanations of why you're unable to assist, you open the door for the other person to offer an alternative to pull you in.

- **Make assertiveness a habit.** If the people in your life know that you will do anything you're asked, the requests will never stop coming. Yes, share your time and energy with others, but don't set a precedent of doing everything just because someone pressures you. When declining invitations, "We have other plans at that time. Thank you for thinking of us," is enough. Remember, when you say Yes to someone else, you may be saying No to your family or to yourself.

In an MSNBC survey, more than
half the workers surveyed said
they feel "overtired and overwhelmed."

Besides the noble art of
getting things done,
there is a noble art of
leaving things undone.

The wisdom of
life consists in the
elimination of
the nonessentials.

—Lin Yutang

Tip 33

Reflect

Some of history's greatest thinkers, from Sir Isaac Newton to Henry David Thoreau, did their best work on a break or sabbatical. I don't think this is an accident or coincidence. Even in their times, as it is in our times, it was difficult to look past the day-to-day distractions and concentrate on the really big mysteries of the universe.

Taking time to reflect on how to solve a problem or how to improve a system often leads to fresh ideas and renewed motivation. You or I may not move into a cabin in the wilderness and devote years to philosophical thinking. Still, we can make time to reflect on the bigger issues in our lives.

A mentor of mine, the former CEO of Dayton-Hudson Corporation (now Target Corp.), got away to a beach house with his wife for two weeks in the spring and two weeks in the fall to reflect, read, think, and be refreshed. He attributes that time to great ideas and longevity as CEO of a large company.

Here are some ideas for making the most of your vacation and reflection time:

- **Leave with an empty desk.** Finish what really needs to be done and then delegate or schedule the rest. By squaring things up before you leave, you will help free your mind of the temptation to focus on work.
- **Get away and be away.** To get the most benefit of your time away from the office, take little or no work with you.
- **Try these breaks.** Take time to walk, think, pray, and be still. Relax. Reflect. Write in a blank journal. Read good books. I love to go to museums, historical sights, and into nature itself. On a more regular basis, getting away to the library, bookstore, or coffee shop can give new perspective, ideas, and rejuvenation.
- **Give yourself enough time.** In the real world, most of us are constrained in how often and how far we can get away. But studies have shown that most of us will spend the first day or two, as well as the last, thinking about work we left behind. So when planning, leave yourself adequate time to relax and unwind.
- **Develop a pattern of reflection.** Try three hours per week and one day per month.

Remember, the really big answers won't always be buried in a memo. Sometimes it takes some fresh air and a few nights rest to find them.

51.2 million Americans, or 35% are "vacation-deprived", earning an average of 14 days and taking 11 of those days, the least amount of vacation days among their international counterparts. —Expedia.com, 2007

Only when
the clamor of the
outside world
is silenced will you
be able to hear
the deeper vibration.
Listen carefully.
—Sarah Ban Breathnach

Tip 34

Habit Change

Aristotle said, "We are all destined by our own habits." What a profound and true statement! Whatever it is you think about the most, you're bound to do the most. And whatever you do the most becomes the story of your day, your week, your year, and your life.

With that in mind, the only way you will have success with the advice in this book is to take what works for you and make it your own. It probably won't be easy at first. Learning new skills is the simple part; breaking out of counterproductive patterns is the tougher part.

In all of my work seeking to help transform people and organizations, I have found two truths. First, positive change is NOT easy. Second, people CAN change for the better in the face of significant challenges. Changing habits takes discipline, focus, and accountability.

Habits don't change on their own, and even with good intentions, they are difficult to alter. If you are serious about changing a habit, take the steps that will create an environment where you can succeed.

I have a friend who lost eighty-five pounds over six months by using some of the following steps to help create a habit-changing environment:

1. **Write down the habit you want to change.** Writing it down solidifies commitment.

2. **List pros and cons.** Note the benefits of changing and the consequences of not changing.

3. **Replace it.** It is easier to "replace" a habit than to "quit" it. For instance, replace watching TV with playing racquetball or reading at the library rather than sitting in your quiet home with the TV off.

4. **Work on one habit at a time.** Some people make so many New Year's resolutions that they get overwhelmed and don't act on any of them. Pick one big habit to change at a time.

5. **Create a clear plan.** Ambiguous goals are not effective.

6. **Break it down.** To avoid feeling overwhelmed, break the plan down into daily actions.

7. **Ask for help.** Create appropriate accountability through a trusted friend or professional. Let the people close to you know you're trying to adopt a significant change. They'll help you carve out the time and motivate you to stick with it. They might even decide to join you!

8. **Reward the target behavior.** Give yourself daily reminders of the new habits you're trying to set, and then reward yourself for performing. For example, give yourself a cup of coffee for keeping your e-mail inbox closed.

9. **Keep it on top of your mind.** Sticky notes or electronic claendar reminders can help you implement your new habit.

10. **Remove distractions.** For example, turn off the e-mail alerts on your smart phone. It is far better for you to answer those e-mails when it fits your schedule than to take them one at a time as they come in.

11. **Make it fun.** Lots of people think of exercise as boring because they associate it with treadmills and crunches. But if you'd rather skip the gym, find something you enjoy like basketball with the kids, a walk with your spouse, or a swim at the pool.

12. **Think long term.** Honestly ask yourself, "What one thing, if I don't stop doing it, will hurt my health over the next ten years?" And then commit: "What one thing will I start doing consistently over the next three months that will enhance my health?"

A nail is driven out by another nail.
Habit is overcome by habit.

—Desiderius Erasmus

Tip 35

People First

Productivity is valuable. Productive people get valuable and important things done. However, I have seen some productivity gurus put productivity *before* people. I have heard some people preach that they will only hold twenty-minute meetings—and they don't.

I like being efficient and effective—with which I have varying degrees of success. Remember, life is about relationships. Getting more work done is great, but it isn't the overall priority of life.

When I was beginning my career, I read a lot of time management and productivity books. One thing that struck me was how they all seemed to think that work was the only goal. I don't subscribe to this brand of thinking. I hope you enjoy your job and become more productive, so that you can succeed and serve people well. But the richest, most fulfilling experiences of our lives come from the moments shared with others. To get the most out of your time, be sure to make room for your family and friends.

I hope you have found this book a useful tool to help you get more out of your days. By using these tips, the hours you gain from your newfound productivity will overshadow the headaches and hassles that come from time to time in our working lives. Remember, your time is a most valuable resource. Spend it wisely. Spend it doing good, productive work. Spend it serving others. When you become efficient and effective on a daily basis, while still valuing relationships, you have an edge—*The Daily Edge*.